# Alpine Meadows

**The stunning beauty of the Rockies' wild flowers**

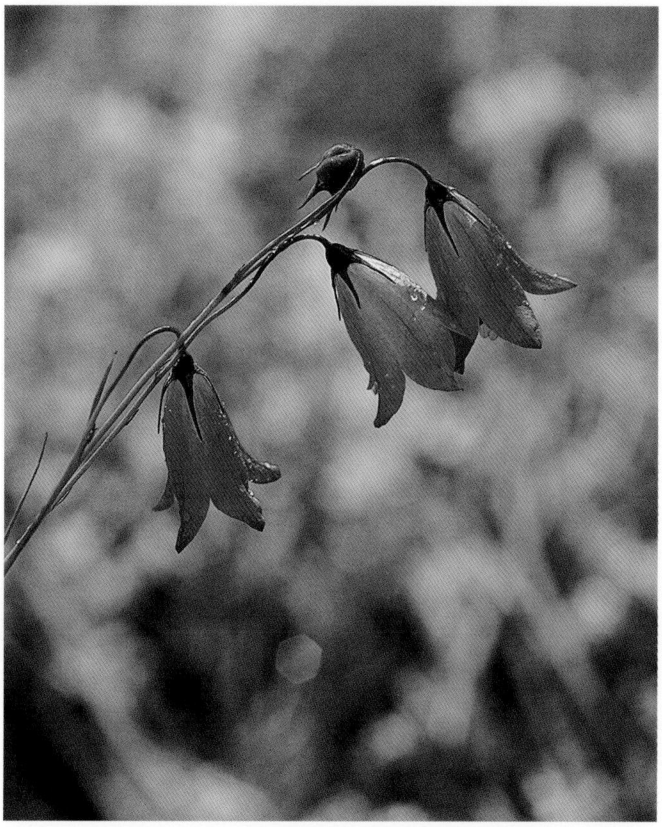

*May the beauty of mountain meadows*
*bring you peace, well being and the inspiration*
*to live a healthy, happy, beautiful life.*

# Alpine Meadows

## The stunning beauty of the Rockies' wild flowers

Dream-like flowers.
Fragrant, gentle flowers.
Flowers of this paradise.
May you please our senses.
Bring joy and nourish our souls.
Vivid you are, and delightful.
A rainbow of living colours.
You are our foremost pride.
Fragrant Canadian flowers.
Delicate, dream-like flowers.

Text and Photographs by
**George Brybycin**

GBP

G B PUBLISHING

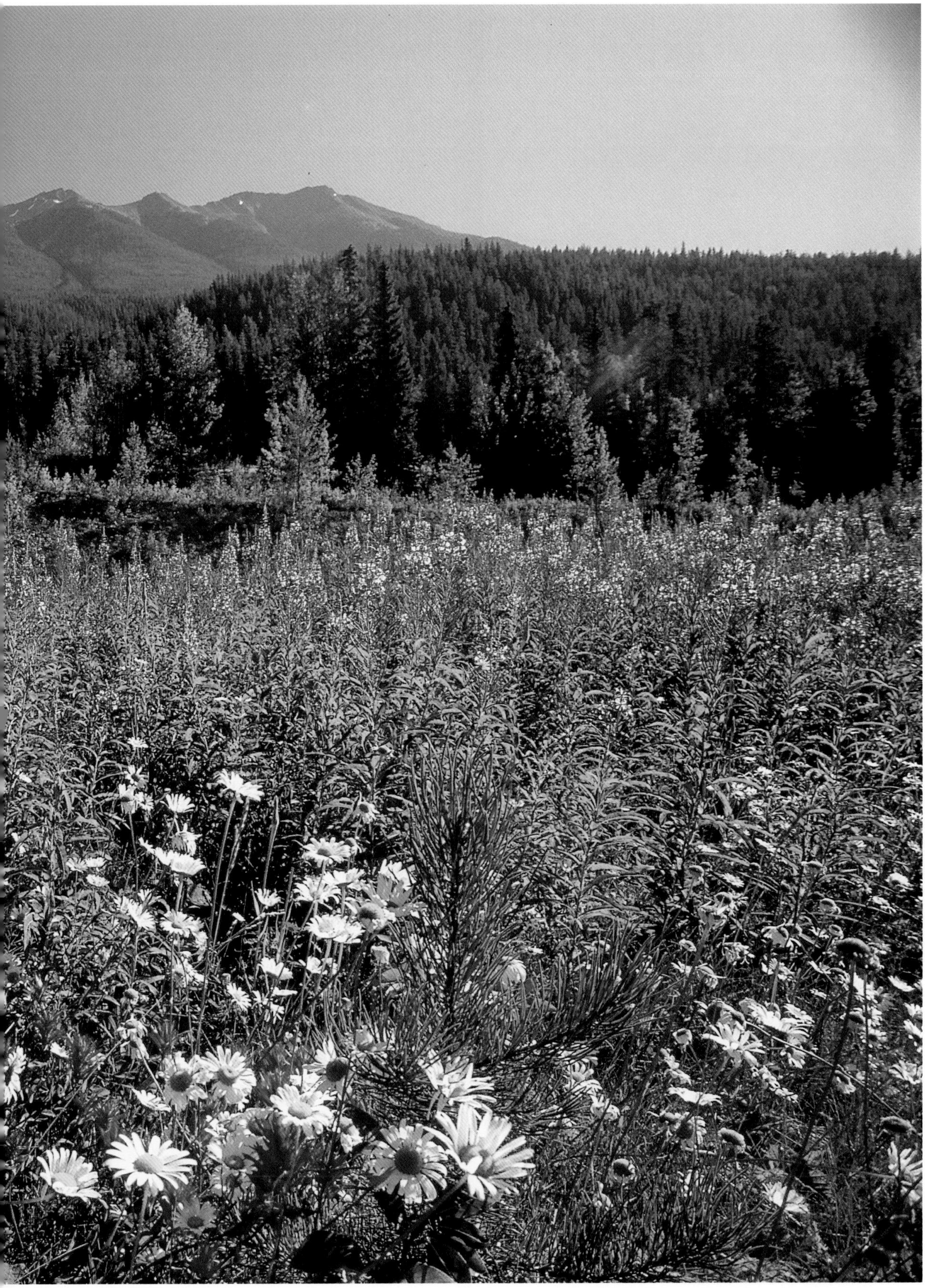

*This colourful palette of mountain meadow sprawls along the Fraser River Valley in Mount Robson Provincial Park. The park protects a large, spectacular wilderness west of the Continental Divide. A milder climate and plenty of precipitation allow for lush forest, plant life and a great variety of fauna. This photograph features the eastern part of the park.*

*If there is a heaven it must look like this heavenly paradise. No tree of life, no serpent, nor Adam and Eve, just these gorgeous, lively fragrant alpine beauties.*

# Introduction

If there is a kingdom of beauty, tranquility and inspiration, it must be high above the treeline in the glorious mountain meadows of the Canadian Rockies; a realm of wild natural beauty and peace.

Protected by its national park status, a large portion of the Canadian Rockies along the Great Divide is probably the most pristine mountain region in the world. Vast in area, but low in population, the Rocky Mountain region is unique: ages old, pristine nature only slightly affected by our modern world.

The Rockies' natural features are many: huge mountains, icefields and glaciers, crystalline emerald lakes, clear water rivers, swift torrents and spectacular waterfalls. A variety of wildlife thrives in the endless green forests that cover the valleys and lower plateaus.

However, the real paradise sprawls above the treeline - the lush green flowering alpine meadows. These meadows come alive in late spring when the first plants hesitantly poke through the snow. First come yellow Glacier Lilies and White Globe-Flowers. Soon, others follow and by early summer the meadows are full of colour, fragrance and life. Insects are busy pollinating flowers and collecting nectar. Rodents and other small mammals now forage on the lush vegetation. Larger animals frequent the meadows and ground nesting birds are busy incubating their eggs.

Later on, in July and August, the meadows explode with spectacular burst of colours provided by red Indian Paintbrushes, yellow Arnicas and blue Asters in full bloom. Dozens of varieties of flowers grow in the meadows all summer long: some grow in colonies; some spread thin and still others pop up as isolated single plants.

In the high mountains above 3000m, where winter is the only season, there is no life. High mountain meadows experience only three months of summer. However, plenty of moisture and sunlight in June, July and August allow plants to grow, bloom and produce seeds in only thirty to forty days. By the end of August, autumn is rapidly advancing and most of the flowers are gone. In September, all the high meadows and alpine tundra turn into fiery reds, yellows and golds as plants, bushes and trees change colours. By the end of September, most of the vegetation is dry; most of the rodents and small mammals have gone into hibernation and the birds have flown south.

Then the silence of the alplands is only sporadically interrupted by the sharp, high-pitched whistle of the Pika (Ochotona princeps), a hardy, non-hibernating dweller in these heights, now busy collecting plant material for food to eat during the long, harsh winter.

At the same time, the majestic Grizzly Bear (Ursus arctos) visits the meadows to dig for the now-sleeping squirrels and rodents which fatten it up before going into hibernation for six months.

In October, the winter is just around the corner. Soon the meadows will begin their peaceful six to seven month rest under a thick, fluffy white blanket of snow.

The only sounds to be heard now, are the howling of the wind and the occasional loud, squeaky cry of Clark's Nutcracker (Nucifraga columbiana) - which, with its quieter cousin, the Gray Jay (Perisoreus canadensis) survive by feeding on the seeds of evergreen tree cones.

Nothing lasts forever, not even the mountain winter, and the cycle of nature turns. By the end of June, the high meadows are once again teeming with rich, eternal life - presenting our eyes with the splendid colours and delicate beauty of wild flowers.

*Grass-of-Parnassus (Parnassia palustris). A humble white star-shaped flower with kidney-shaped leaves. It is found in dense colonies in mossy wet places, along alpine brooks or snowbeds at or above the timberline.*

*Venus's Slipper (Calypso bulbosa) is a perennial herb and one of the smallest of the orchid family. It is found chiefly on the damp floor of Lodgepole Pine forest. This exquisitely showy beauty flowers for a very short time in early summer.*

*Brown-eyed Susan (Gaillardia aristata). This humble, pleasant-looking herb is found in sunny, dry areas of the south-central foothills. The perennial flower reaches 50 cm in height and 5 cm in diameter (above).*

*This incredible green paradise sprawls along the Bow Summit, Banff National Park. Most of the Rocky Mountain flowers can be found here, from early June to early September. Draped in haze are Mt. Hector (3394m) on the left and Bow Peak (2868m) on the right. (left)*

*This splendid alpine meadow in the Rocky Mountains is dominated by Indian Paintbrush (Castilleja miniata),Compound-leaved Flea-Bane (Erigeron compositus) -related to genus Aster, Heart-leaved Arnica (Arnica cordifolia), Valerian (Valeriana sitchensis) and many others.*

*Colonized almost entirely by White Pasque Flower (Pulsatilla occidentalis) and a few Indian Paintbrushes, this green, carpet-like meadow of the central Rockies is rich and healthy - indicating an undisturbed ecosystem.*

*White Globe-Flower (Trollius albiflorus) is a creamy white harbinger of spring, often poking through the snow in early summer. Found along sub-alpine and alpine brooks and snowbeds, it grows in masses - small and large clumps. (above)*

*Lower Waterfowl Lake is an emerald jewel along the Mistaya River. In the center of the photo, Chephren Lake nestles at the foot of Howse Peak, surrounded by healthy, green forest. Banff National Park. (left)*

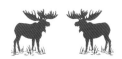

One of the better known landmarks of the Rockies - the Valley of the Ten Peaks, Banff National Park. The golden Alberta autumn at its best: snowy, jagged peaks, cobalt blue Alberta skies and the fiery orange of Mountain Ash. This is Alberta in all her glory.

*This is White Pasque Flower (Pulsatilla occidentalis) country. It favours mostly moist slopes and snowy hollows above the timberline. Often called "towhead babies" because of their fuzzy-shaggy blond heads in fruiting phase.*

*Lush alpine meadows sprawl around Rock Isle Lake in the southeastern corner of Kootenay National Park. This area is shared by man and beast.Plenty of wildlife live here including: Grizzly bear, deer, elk, cougars and wolves.*

*Geraldine Valley in Jasper National Park is a very special place.
The diversity of landscapes is great,and include several large waterfalls,
three large lakes, rich forest and colourful alpine meadows.
A rough access trail keep tourism at bay so the area is relatively intact.*

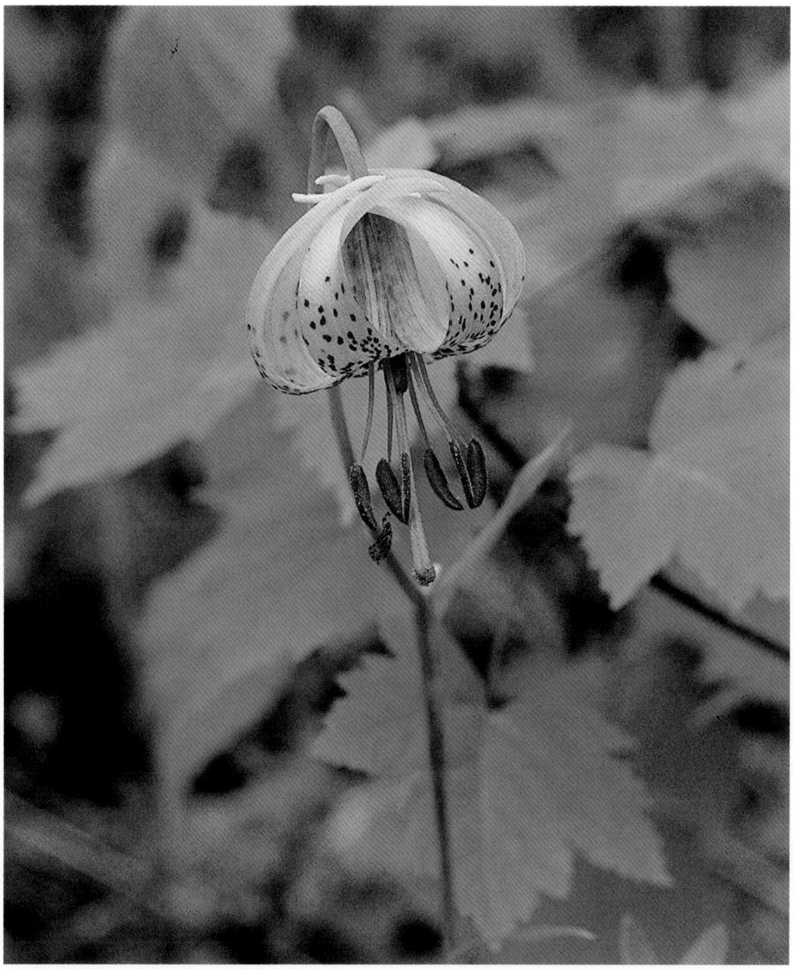

*Tiger lily (Lilium columbianum). Liliacae, the lily family, comprises mostly herbaceous plants of nearly 30 species. Some are as tall as 50 cm and some are known to be poisonous. Most are flamboyant and their calyx and corolla are coloured. Most lilies are of gentle, delicate build and are a most pleasant sight.*

*As devastating as it might seem, forest fires are actually a blessing for the environment. Enriched by the ashes, the soil is more productive. More light and rain penetrate the area and where dark forest once was, green forest floor and meadow emerges. Here a rich crop of Smooth Aster (Aster leavis) enjoy the sunny, open spaces. (above)*

*Bright Fireweed (Epilobium angustifolium) is commonly seen flowering along roads, railways and fire clearings. It thrives in disturbed soil and reaches over a meter in height. It ascends far above the timberline to alpine meadows and prefers sunny, sheltered slopes where it reaches only 20 - 30 cm in height. (left)*

*A happy herd of elk (Cervus elaphus) enjoy a sunny summer morning. The harsh climate of the Rockies provides only four months of green pasture; two months of spring and fall when pickings are less and 5 - 6 long, cold months of winter when life is very hard and escaping predators in deep snow is more difficult.*

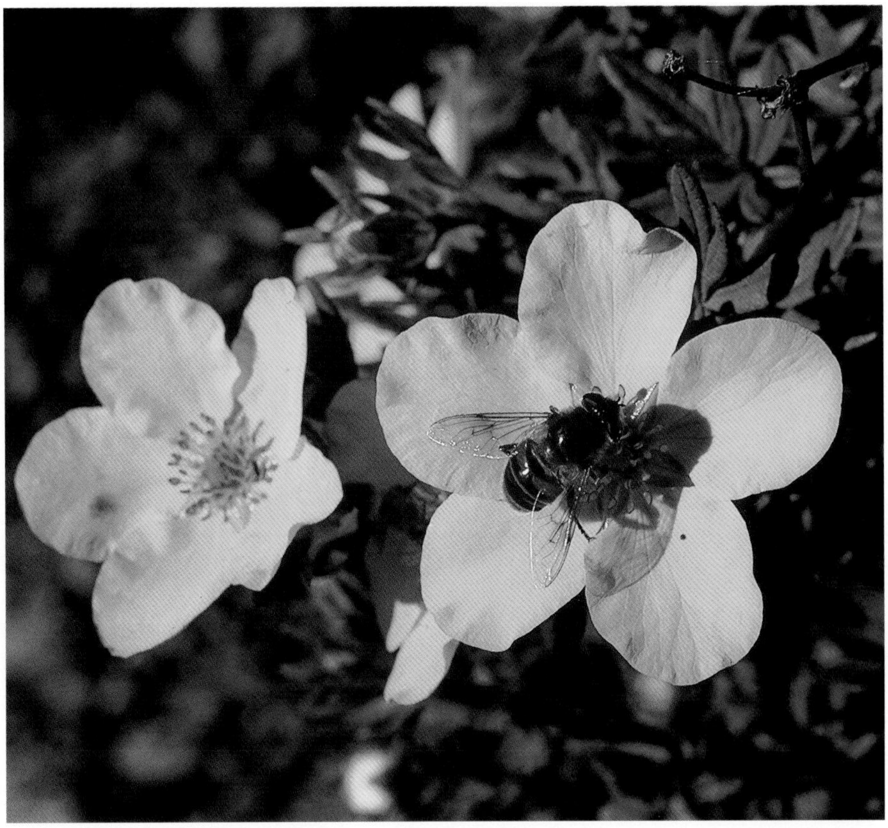

*Shrubby Cinquefoil (Potentilla fruticosa). This shrub is very diversified in size, depending on where it grows. In its preferred calcareous soil, it may reach 150 cm in height. On poor, rocky soil it might only reach 30 - 40 cm. Its bright yellow flowers are solitary or few together. It can be found in wet, dry and rocky soils and reaches well above the timberline.*

## Flowers and more flowers

The following list names the most common flowers found in the meadows of the Canadian Rocky Mountains. This is but a small fraction of the varieties to be found there. The location of these flowers will vary due to altitude and latitude. For example, a specific type of flower might grow at an elevation of 2400 m in Waterton and only 2000 m in Jasper because of climate differences. Bear Grass and Monkey Flower are found only in the extreme south. The Yellow Lady's Slipper is extinct in the more heavily used areas of the Rockies, notably around Banff, due to illegal picking.

The National Parks Act clearly stipulates that picking flowers and other plants, removing any objects like wood, rock, fossils or anything else is against the law and strictly prohibited.

Indian Paintbrush (Castilleja miniata)
Fireweed (Epilobium angustifolium)
Broad-leaved Willow-Herb (Epilobium latifolium)
Yellow Columbine (Aquilegia flavescens)
Western Wood Lily (Lilium montanum)
Glacier Lily (Erythronium grandiflorum)
Bear Grass (Xerophyllum tenax)
Shooting Star (Dodecatheon pauciflorum)
Yellow Lady's Slipper (Cypripedium calceolus)
Venus's Slipper (Calypso bulbosa)
Franklin's Lady's Slipper (Cypripedium passerinum)
Alpine Harebell (Campanula lasiocarpa)
Common Harebell (Campanula rotundifolio)
Prairie Crocus (Pulsatilla Ludoviciana)
White Globe-Flower (Trollius albiflorus)
Heart-leaved Arnica (Arnica cordifolia)
Smooth Aster (Aster laevis)
Golden Flea-Bane (Erigeron aureus)
Compound-leaved Flea-Bane (Erigeron compositus)
Flea-Bane (Erigeron peregrinus)
Brown-eyed Susan (Gaillardia aristata)
Wild Rose (Rosa woodsii)
Shrubby Cinquefoil (Potentilla fruticosa)
Yellow Mountain Avens (Dryas Drummondii)
White-flowered Mountain Avens (Dryas Hookeriana)
White Pasque Flower (Pulsatilla occidentalis)
Bunchberry (Cornus canadensis)
Alpine Forget-me-not (Myosotis alpestris)
Bird's-Eye Primrose (Primula mistassinica)
Early Blue Violet (Viola adunca)
Yellow Violet (Viola orbiculata)
Valerian (Valeriana sitchensis)
Yarrow (Achillea nigrescens)
Woolly Everlasting (Antennaria lanata)
Pearly Everlasting (Anaphalis margaritacea)
Groundsel (Senecio triangularis)
Rocky Mountain Dandelion (Taraxacum scopulorum)
Rocky Mountain Goldenrod (Solidago multiradiata)
Twin Flower (Linnaea borealis)
Butterwort (Penguicula vulgaris)
Elephant's Head (Pedicularis greonlandica)
Lousewort (Pedicularis contorta)
Lungwort (Mertensia paniculata)
Bracted Wintergreen (Pyrola bracteata)
One-flowered Wintergreen (Moneses uniflora)
Yellow Mountain Saxifrage (Saxifraga aizoides)
White Camas (Zygadenus elegans)
Yellow Mountain Heath (Phyllodoce glandulifera)
Purple Mountain Heath (Phyllodoce empetriformis)
Mountain Heather (Cassiope Mertensiana)
Moss Campion (Silene acaulis)
Grass-of-Parnassus (Parnassia fimbriata)
Eschscholtz's Buttercup (Ranunculus Eschscholtzii)
Bladder Locoweed (Oxytropis podocarpa)
Yellow Monkey Flower (Mimulus guttatus)
Red Monkey Flower (Mimulus Lewisii)

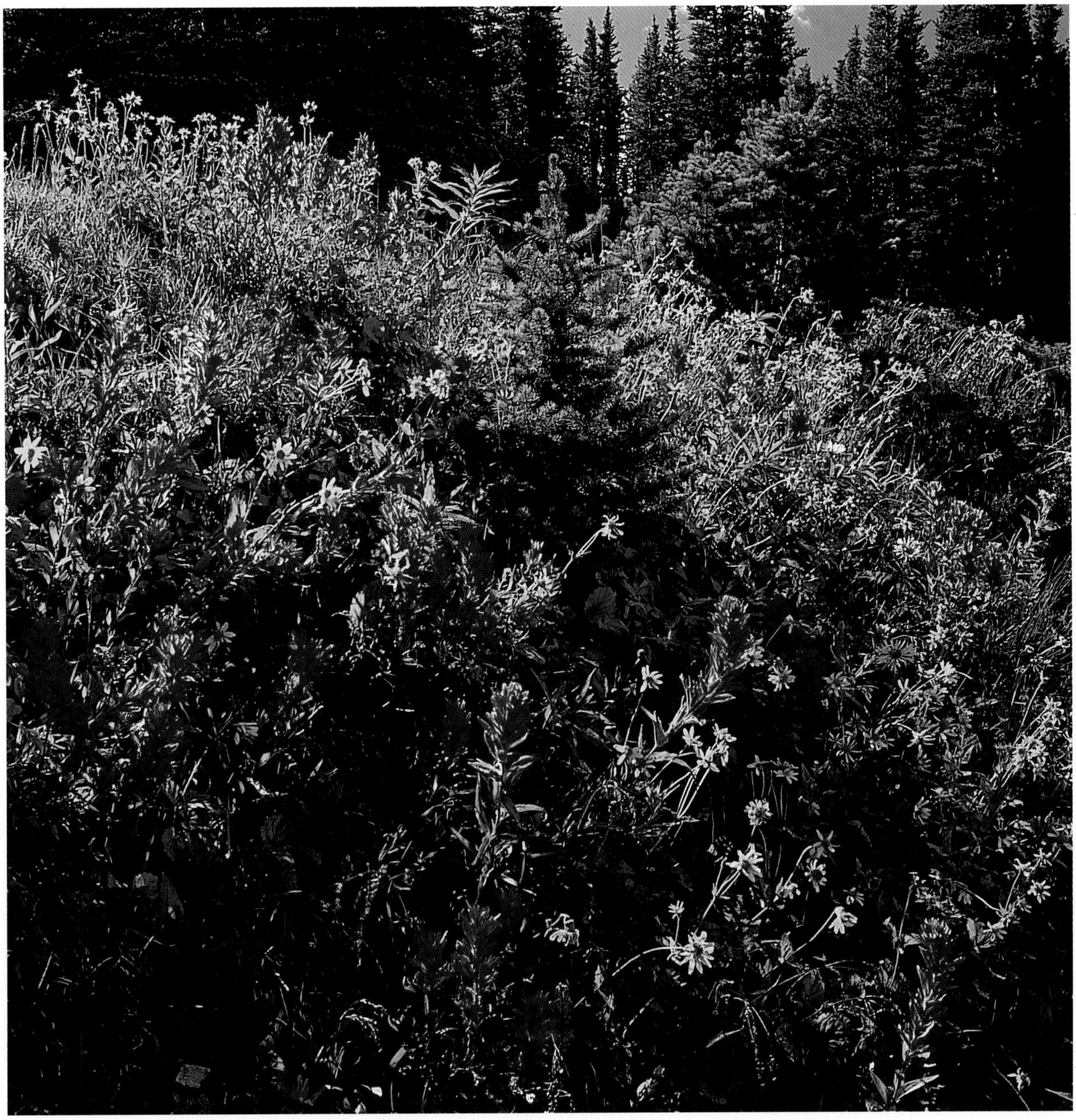

*This paradisaical high mountain meadow is unmatched by any man-made creation. The stunning variety of shapes and colours, and the dazzling array of fragrances is simply overwhelming. May this mountain meadow's beauty remain in your heart and soul for the rest of your days.*

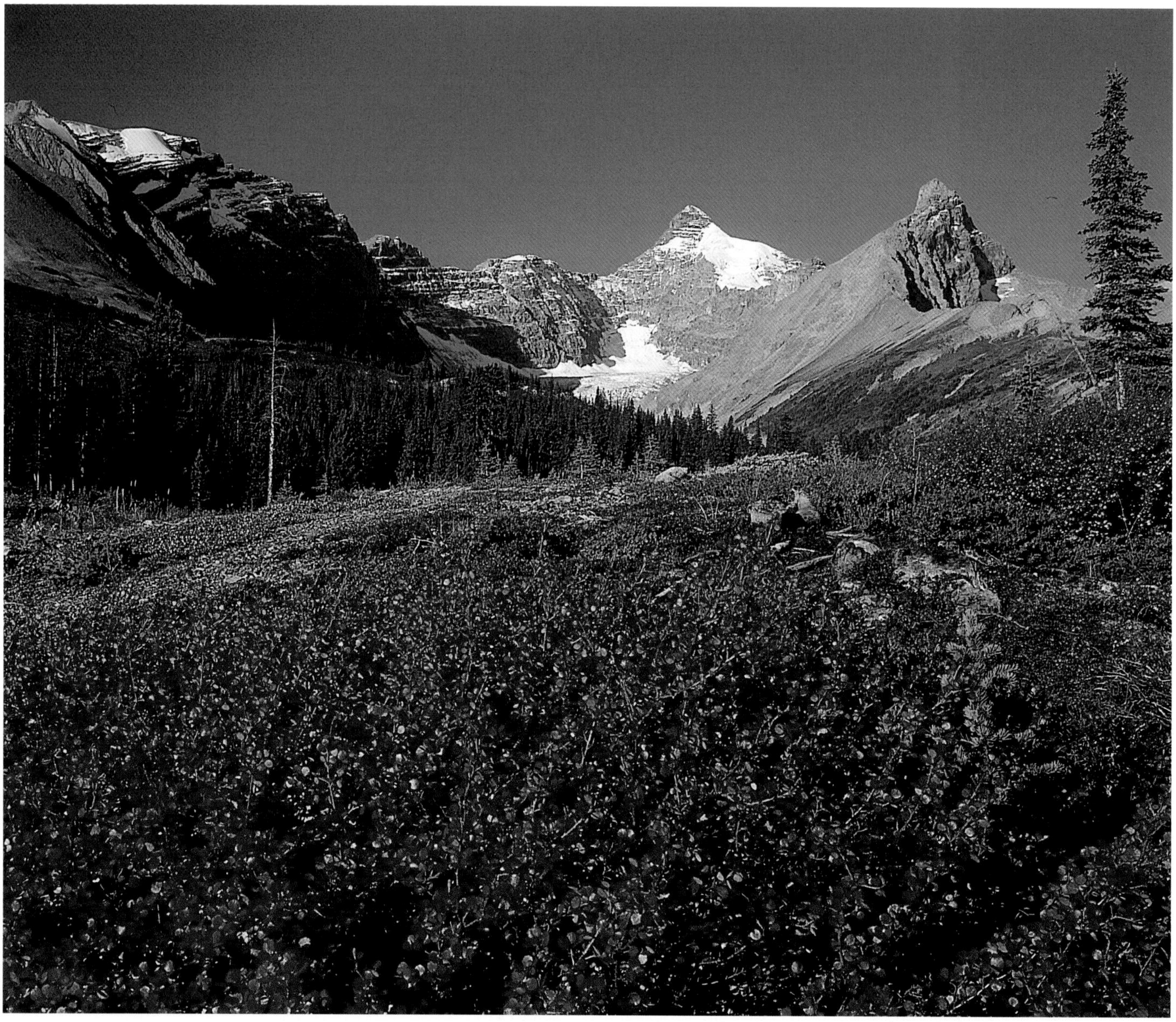

*Stunning fiery colours of the alpine autumn by the Sunwapta Pass near Mt. Athabasca. Banff/Jasper National Parks.*

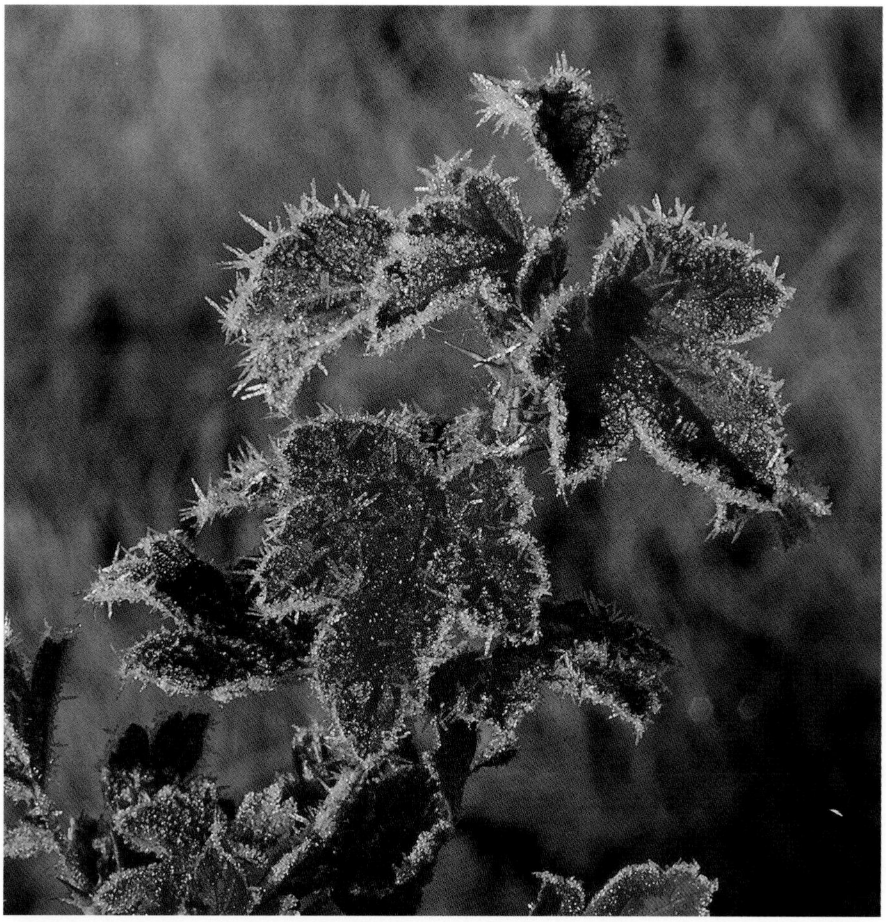

*A frosted shrub of Wild Goose Berry on a late autumn morning. If one can see the world of beauty in a humble little flower, the intricate patterns on a plant's leaf, or a frost decorated bush, one is a special sort of human. The farther one moves from the materialistic world into nature's treasures, the richer and more humane one becomes.*

As awesome as it seems,
the Grizzly is a gentle beast:
wild, independent and free.
The Grizz is reasonably tolerant.
Knowing who is who -
that's nature's law.
Stay at a safe distance and
perhaps the Grizz will make
a meal of something else.
The Grizz is a gentle beast -
but unpredictable, too!

*The Grizzly Bear (Ursus arctos), the undisputed monarch of the Canadian wilderness. The grizzly's tame look and slow movements are misleading. This is an extremely unpredictable animal: fast and dangerous; capable of killing the largest moose, elk or caribou. What chance would a mere human have when confronting such a giant? If you spot a grizzly, leave the area quickly. If surprised by a bear, climb a tree as high and fast as you can. When attacked, use pepper spray or play dead. Fighting back will only irritate the bear and prompt a more severe result. Every year, people are severely injured or killed by bears in the wilderness. Avoid becoming one of them.*

*Oregon Grapes (Berberis repens). This dwarf creeping shrub bears berry-like fruit and is found in the warmer southwestern parts of the Rockies. The fruit is quite delicious after the first or second frost.*

*A look at Banff National Park's Valley of the Ten Peaks from a different angle. The stark majesty of the rugged peaks, the gentle beauty of mountain flowers and the variety of landscapes make this area a dream-like paradise of nature.*

The monarch of the heights, the Bighorn Sheep (Ovis canadensis) is a close relative of the Dall Sheep and Stone's Sheep of North America. It inhabits mountains from the Alberta and British Columbia Rockies right down to Mexico.

*Yellow Lady's Slipper (Cypripedium calceolus) is a perennial fragrant herb, it reaches an average height of 20 cm. It flowers in early summer in the lower, dryer valleys, both in the open and in the forest.*

## Ode to the Lady Slipper

You were the lady of our choice.
You were more refined, elegant
and flamboyant than any lady we had known.
Your beauty was legendary, gentle and unmatched.
Your fragrance was gentle, natural and mysterious.
You were the First Lady of green meadows;
the rain, wind and sun were your friends.
You brought us uniquely profound joy and fun.
You were. You are no more. You are gone.
In many places you grew gracefully.
You are extinct. Exterminated now.
We bid you farewell, great lady of our joy;
We hope that you will return someday.
We do not want our lives to be sad and empty.
Please come back, o gorgeous lady
of the meadows. Soon!

*Along the trail to Mt. Assiniboine near the Citadel Pass, the meadows are green and lush, and the area is frequented by a rich variety of fauna including the Grizzly Bear. Banff National Park.*

*East of Mt. Edith Cavell, Cavell Meadows put on a colourful display each summer. Regardless of the high altitude and northern latitude, the flowers are as gorgeous and plentiful as in the south. Jasper National Park.*

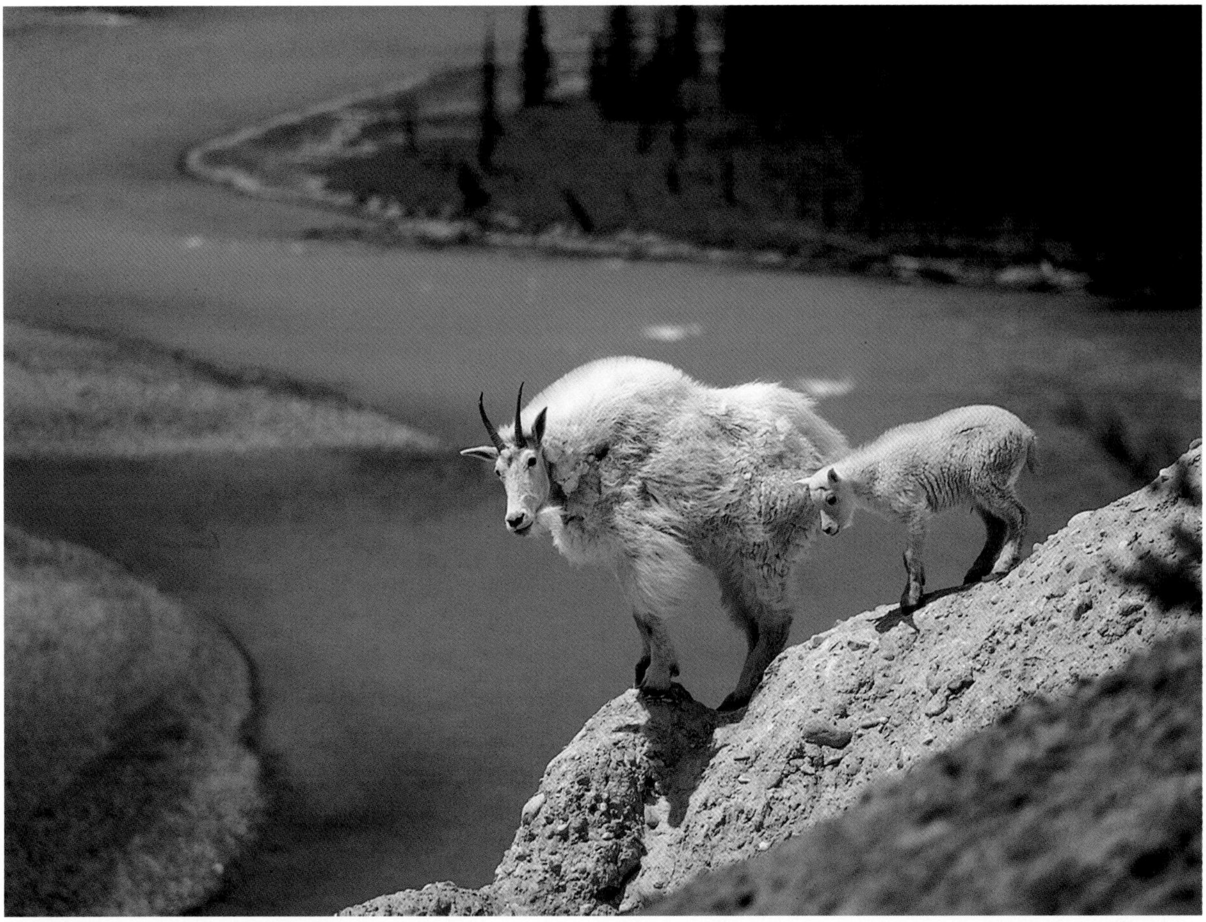

*A fearless mountain acrobat - the Mountain Goat (Oreamnos americanus) overlooking the Athabasca River in Jasper National Park. It inhabits the mountains of the northwest from Alaska to Montana. (above)*

*The grandeur of veil-like Tangle Falls. Jasper National Park. The water comes from a large snowfield on the north side of Tangle Peak. (left)*

*Pearly Everlasting (Anaphalis margaritacea), a tufted perennial herb 15 - 20 cm tall. It grows in clusters in rather stony, dry sub-alpine areas. There are almost a dozen varieties of the Everlasting genus in North America, in varying climatic zones.*

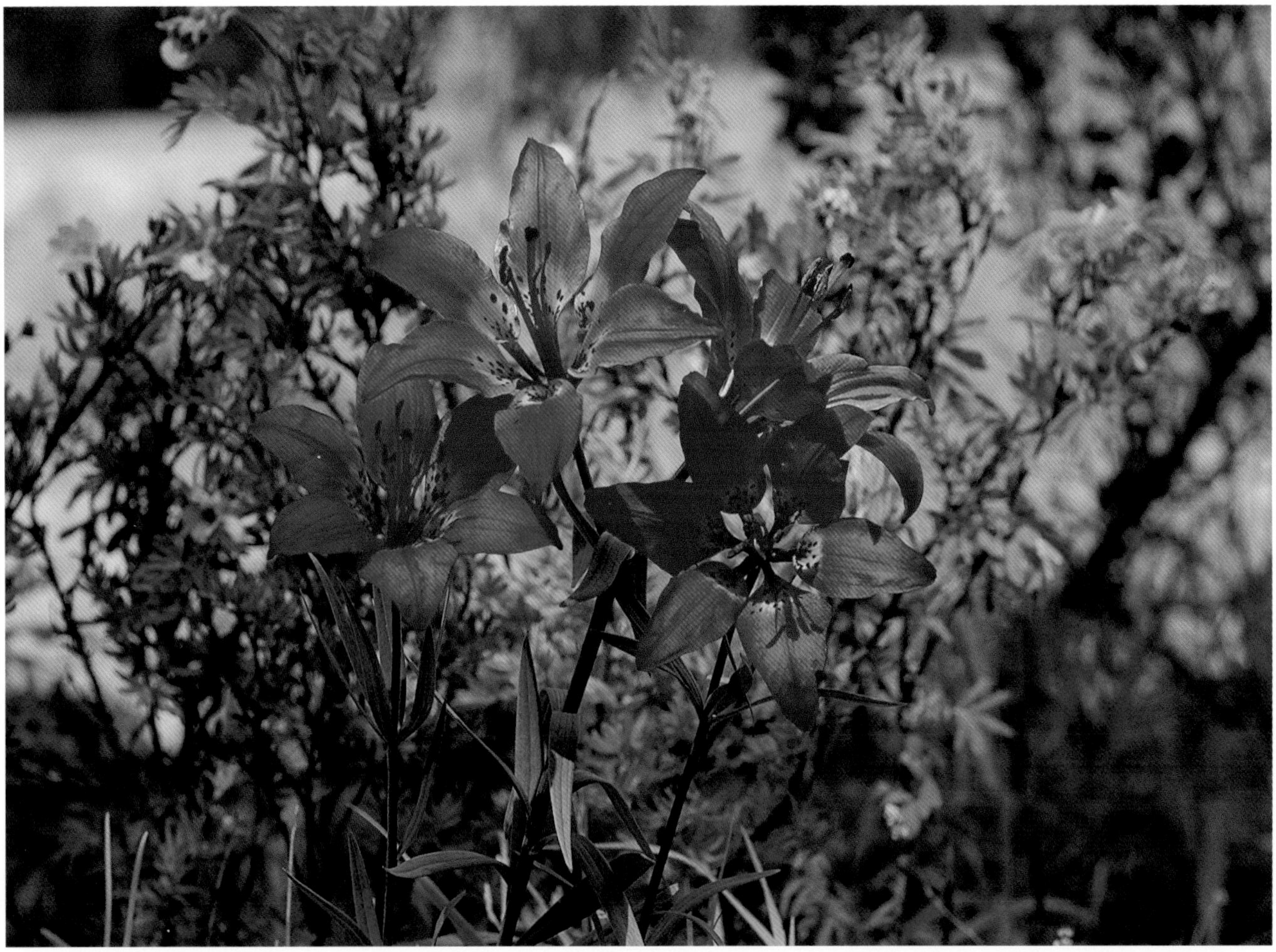

*Western Wood Lily(Lilium montanum) is a showy perennial beauty 40 - 50 cm in height, flowering in early summer. It usually grows individually- one flower to a stem with an occasional plant bearing two or three flowers. Its preferred homes are the semi-moist, subalpine meadows and the forest floor.*

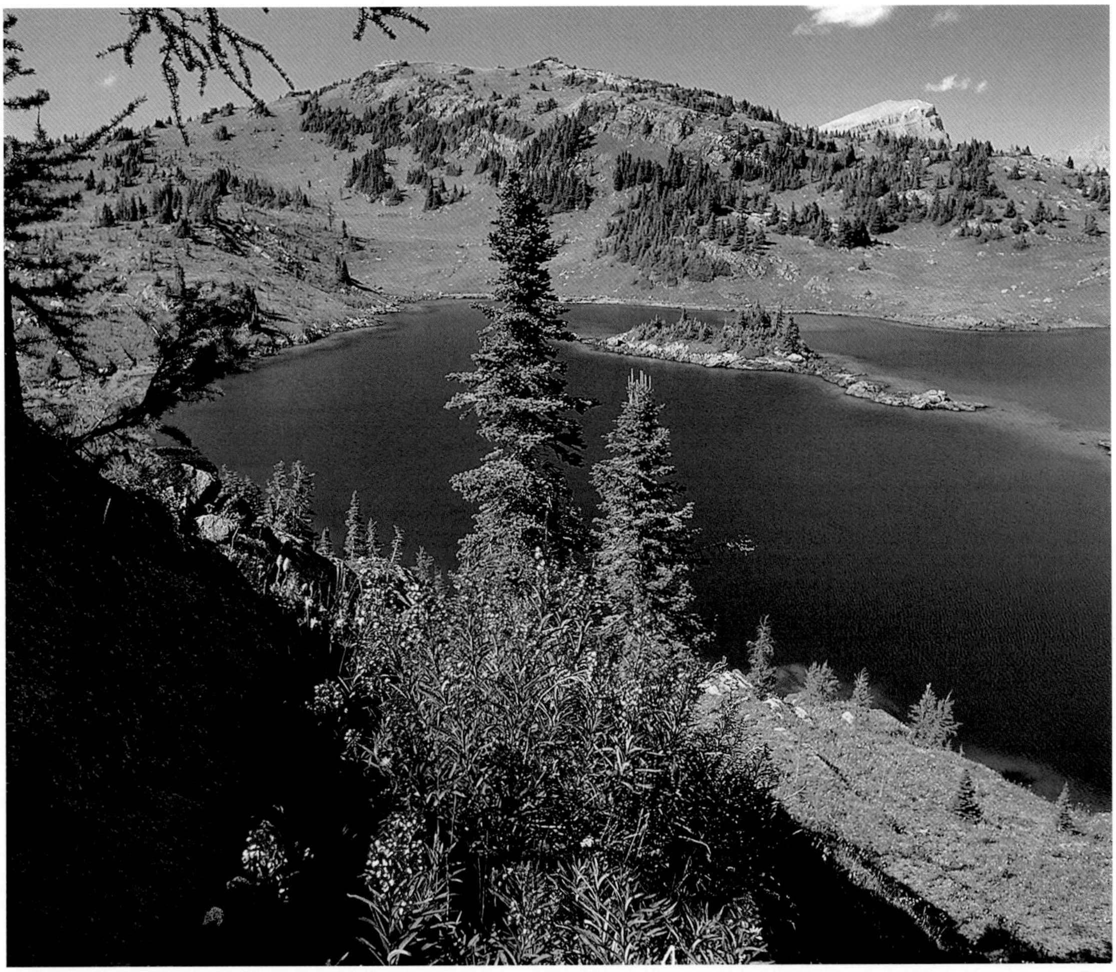

*Rock Isle Lake, Kootenay National Park, is located in the heart of spectacular wilderness. High altitude Fireweed (Epilobium angustifolium)is barely 30 cm tall, but is as beautiful as the ones growing at lower elevations. (above)*

*Angel Glacier hangs on the northern face of Mt. Edith Cavell in Jasper National Park. The cluster of tall, bright yellow Ragwort (Senecio triangularis) form a pleasant foreground. (left)*

*For a Mule Deer (Odocoileus hemionus) a mountain meadow is just the place to dine - a source of gourmet food. In theory, animals have no sense of beauty, or, indeed, any use for it. Why then, do so many animals wear spectacularly beautiful colours and patterns? To attract the opposite sex? Perhaps the theories are wrong and animals are sensitive to beauty. (above)*

*Rejuvenated by a forest fire, enriched by ashes, the soil allows rich new plantlife to flourish. The sunloving Heart - leaved Arnica (Arnica cordifolia) has found a hospitable home here. (left)*

# The National Parks Concept

Since the most beautiful parts of the Canadian Rockies are located in National Parks, it would be wise to mention what they are for, as well as how and why they came to be.

Bless the wisdom and noble efforts of our forefathers for envisioning the need to protect the pristine beauty of nature and its inhabitants over one hundred years ago - well before there was any real threat to them.

The concept of National Parks was born in the United States of America and was first realized in the creation of Yellowstone National Park in 1872. Canada followed suit, creating Banff National Park in 1885. Over many years, the park was enlarged to reach today's size of 6,641 square km. Four other National Parks were also created in the Rockies: Jasper, Kootenay, Waterton and Yoho, and were regulated by the National Parks Act of 1930.

The original Act described the purpose of National Parks in this way: "The National Parks are hereby dedicated to the people of Canada for their benefit, education and enjoyment, subject to this Act and the regulations and the National Parks shall be maintained and made use of so as to leave them unimpaired for the enjoyment of future generations." (R.S., c.N - 13, s.1)

The parks were meant to be a public possession, which means that you and I could enjoy them at any time. The Act, like too many legal documents, is too general and contains many loopholes. Over time, several amendments to the Act were implemented - including more loopholes, giving more authority to local administrators in the making of major decisions. This resulted in a drastic change in the direction Parks are going, and seriously eroded the original concept of National Parks.

The Act says "leave them unimpaired" - meaning pristine, natural, undisturbed. Yet, some parts of our Parks are now built up and paved over until they resemble big, noisy, polluted cities rather than National Parks. Now they face polluted rivers, creeks and lakes.

Hundreds of animals are killed each year by the growing, out of control traffic in the Parks. Some species of animals and plants are near extinction in our "protected" National Parks.

What has happened? Pecunia non olet?

We must decide now, whether we want National Parks or amusement parks!

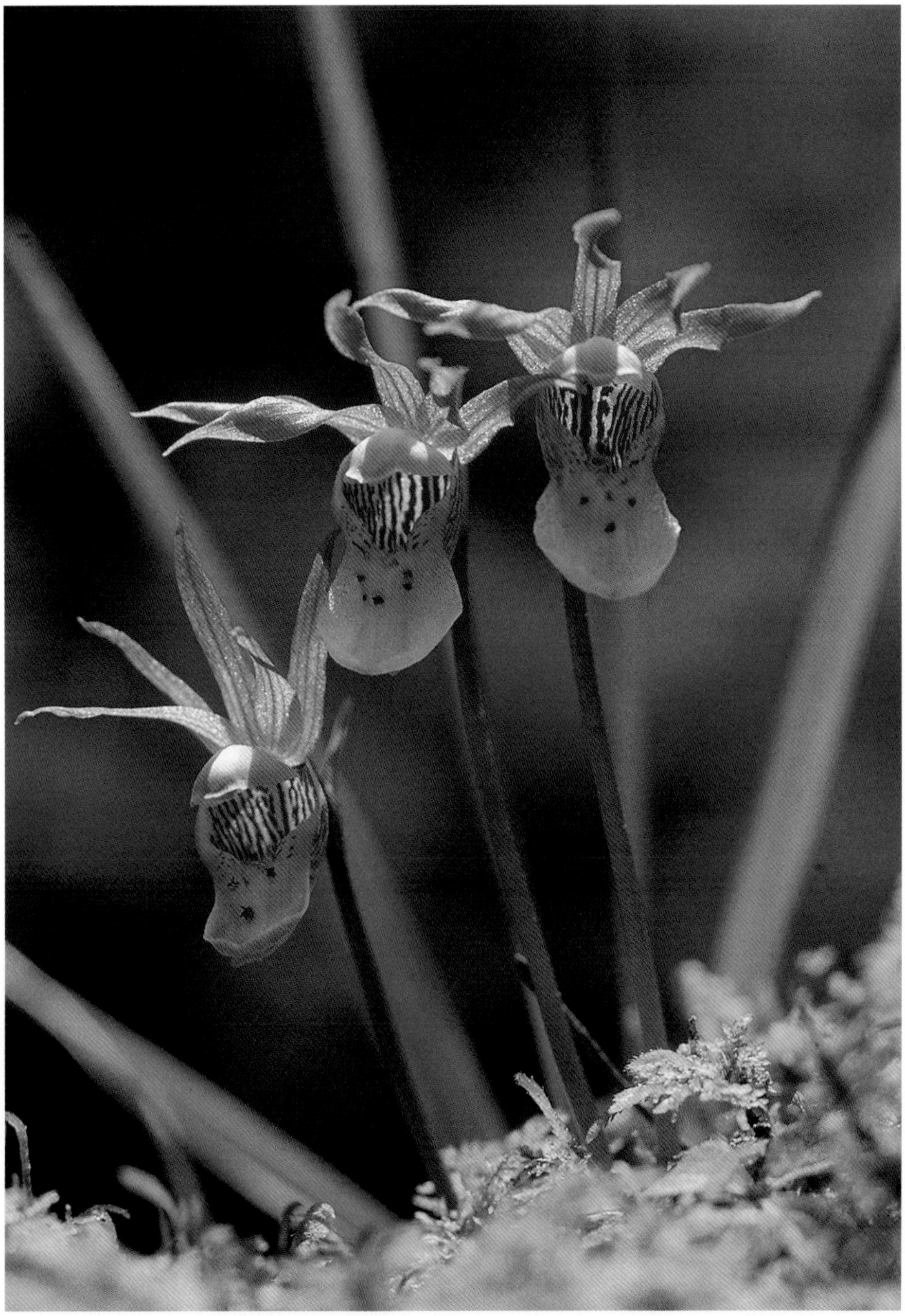

*The most exquisite and elusive of North American orchids, Venus's Slipper (Calypso bulbosa) flowers in early summer and is found growing singly as well as in both large and small clusters. It prefers the damp forest floor of the Lodgepole Pine. Look at them, enjoy their fragrance, but never, ever pick them. They are too beautiful, too innocent to be destroyed. Also, they must mature through their full cycle in order to reproduce and continue to flourish.*

*Where are you rushing, clear white water? To bring life to thirsty flowers, mosses, animals and birds. Evaporated from the deep blue oceans, your journey takes you high over the blue skies to the tops of lofty mountains. Then you pour down the green slopes, generously providing life to all. What an interesting life you lead, oh vital cool, clear water!*

*Yellow Columbine (Aquilegia flavescens) is one of the prettiest flowers of the Rockies. Depending on the elevation, its flowering stem varies from 25 to 55 cm, it grows to just above the timberline. The red-flowered variety prefers moist alpine meadows and damp upper forest. (above)*

*The extremely lush vegetation on the eastern slopes of Wapta Mountain, Yoho National Park, is blessed with both plenty of rain and a glacier to provide a steady flow of water all summer long. This is an avalanche area and trees have no chance to survive here. (left)*

*At home in the Rockies, Elk or Wapiti (Cervus elaphus) spend the summer in the forest or meadows but winter in the lower, windswept valleys. Have you ever watched an animal forage in a meadow? A leaf here, a flower there - never eating the entire plant or stripping a tree of all its leaves. Conserve for tomorrow, wise environmentalist. (above)*

*A heartwarming "bouquet" of Compound-leaved Flea-Bane (Erigeron compositus) of the Aster genus and some Arnicas enjoy the sun-bathed slopes of an alpine meadow. (left)*

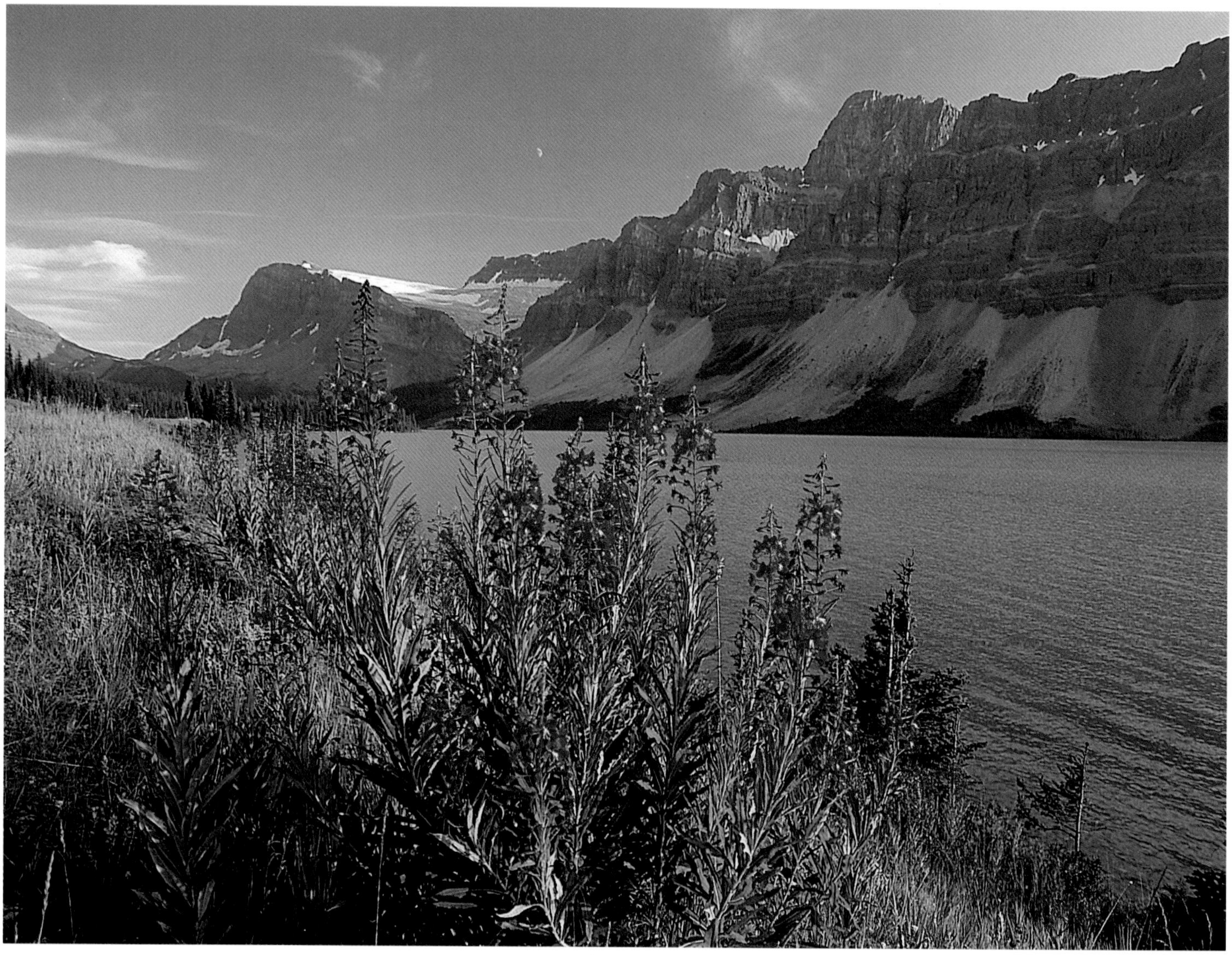

*Bow Lake, Banff National Park, is located just below Bow Glacier - a source of the Bow River, winding down east through the central Rockies. The emerald water of the lake is due to glacial silt from Bow Glacier and the large Wapta Icefield to the south.*

*The Prairie Crocus (Pulsatilla Ludoviciana) is a true harbinger of spring. It flowers on sunny slopes in May and June, when snow is still on the ground. It is found mostly along the plains, the foothills and lower mountains - north to the Arctic Coast, the Yukon and eastern Alaska.*

*Arnica is a large genus in the Canadian Rockies with around a dozen species found near the timberline. Heart-leaved Arnica (Arnica cordifolia) is one of the prettiest perennial herbs with its bright yellow colour in various shades. It is commonly found in coniferous forest and occasionally in alpine meadows. (above)*

*The dazzling bright Yellow Mountain Saxifrage (Saxifraga aizoides), one of a large genus with dozens of species in the Rockies alone. It is found along gravel bars and creeks up to well above the timberline. Sharing the neighbourhood with Saxifrage, is Broad-leaved Willow-Herb (Epilobium latifolium) which enjoys precisely the same moist environment. (left)*

*There are seven major groups of the Sciuridae Squirrel family in the world. One of the more attractive and vivacious is the Golden-mantled Ground Squirrel (Spermophilus lateralis) which is commonly found throughout the Rockies. (above)*

*The world-famous Lake Louise and the monumental Mt. Victoria (3464m), Banff National Park, comprise this pleasant summer scene. In the foreground are Shrubby Cinquefoil (Potentilla fruticosa) and a tiny ground squirrel. (left)*

*A showy herb of the wet Broad-leaved Willow-Herb (Epilobium latifolium) which is common throughout the region. (upper)*

*One of the showiest alpine flowers is the Red Monkey-Flower (Mimulus Lewisii). In the Rockies, it grows exclusively in Waterton Lakes National Park. (lower)*

*The Western Wood Lily (Lilium montanum) shares space with the Wild Rose (Rosa woodsii). They both require similar growing conditions. (upper)*

*A prickly shrub common throughout Alberta and lower parts of the Rockies, the Wild Rose (Rosa woodsii) is the official flower of Alberta. (lower)*

*The Bear Grass (Xerophyllum tenax) is a unique herb, resembling no other flower. This creamy white, smooth pernnial blums gradually from the bottom up, reaching a maximum of 1.5 m tall. In the Rockies, it is found in the Waterton area only and grows best on sunny, dry slopes, mostly in the subalpine zone. (above)*

*A misty, moody, colourful morning in the meadow near the Valley of the Ten Peaks in Banff National Park. Mountain meadows are so captivating with their beauty that it is easy to become addicted; to get a pure natural high from the fragrance of the wilderness. Hike the trails here and experience the healing powers of nature. (left)*

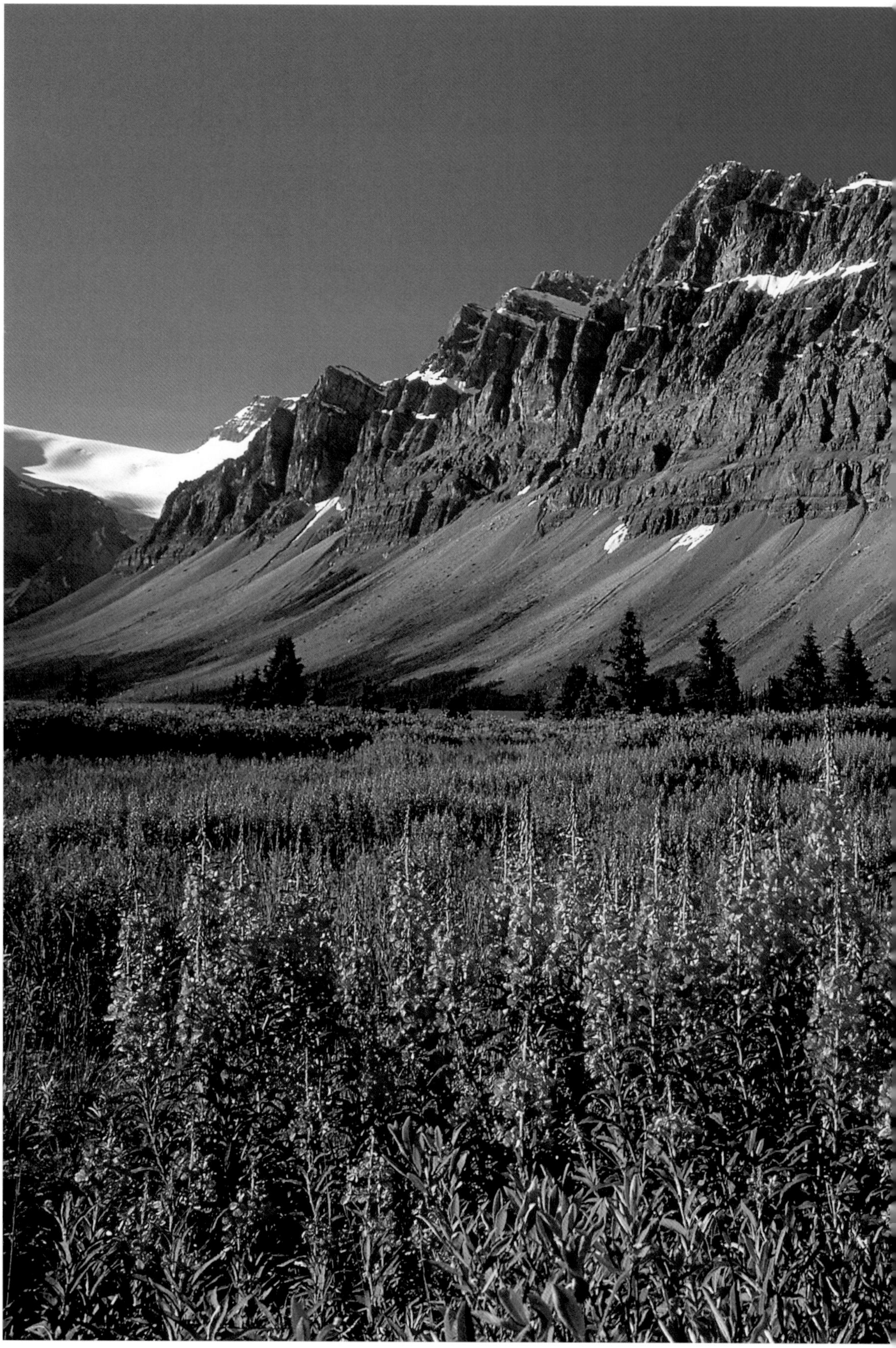

*This sub-alpine tundra surrounds the Bow Lake area, near the source of the Bow River. The hardy yet showy Fireweed (Epilobium angustifolium) grows in diversified regions from the low valleys to alpine meadows as high as 2500 m. The mountain in the background is the northern peak of Crowfoot Mountain (3050m). Banff National Park.*

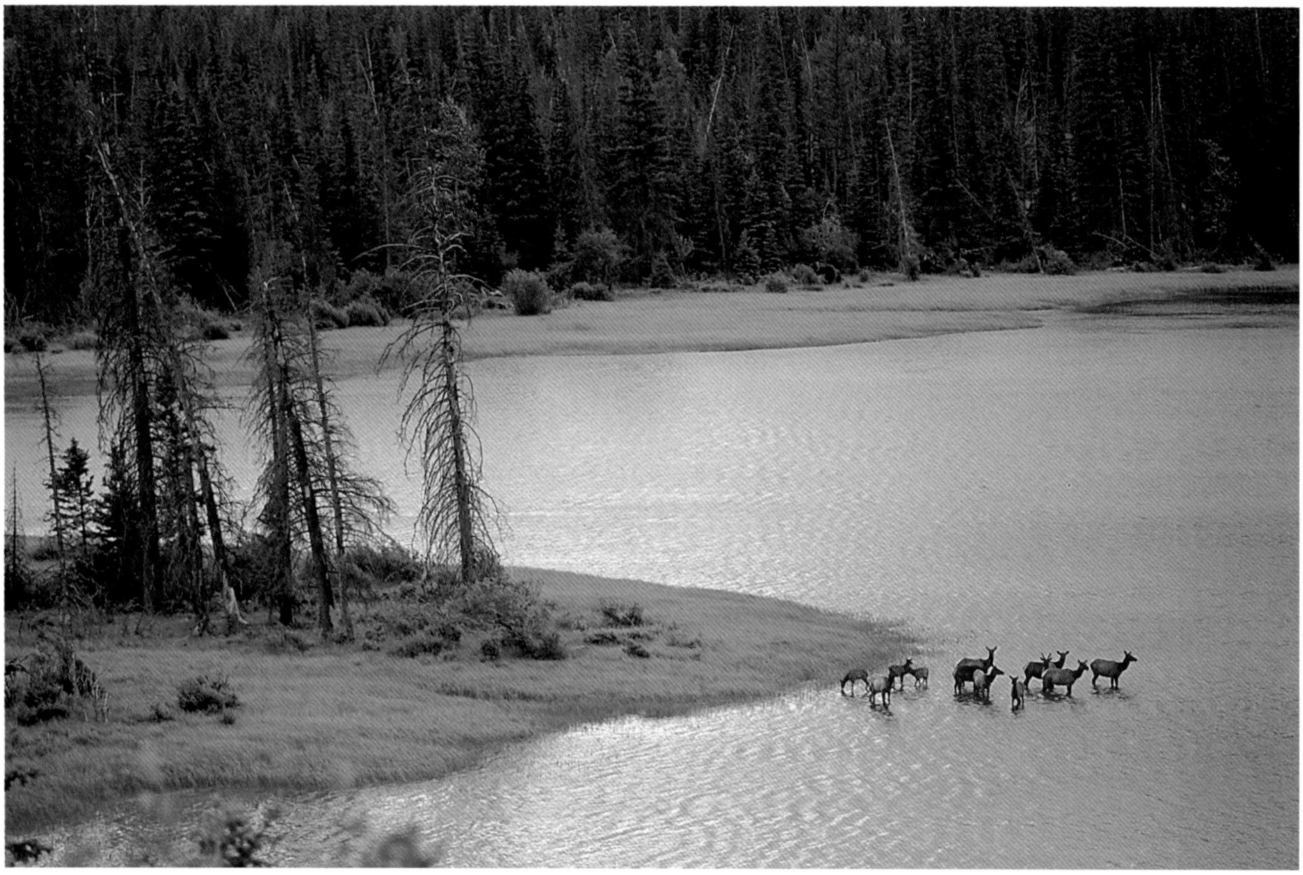

*Elk, or Wapiti (Cervus elaphus), often seek safety in the water or on an island, if available. In calving season, cows retreat to the island and stay there long enough to allow their young to become strong enough to run. Major predators, like wolves, cougars and coyotes hate to get their fancy furs wet unless they have to. (above)*

*Jasper National Park's Geraldine Valley abounds with many natural features: lakes, falls, forest, meadows, and a great variety of flowers. The area is blessed with ample rainfall and thus is rich with green nature. (right)*

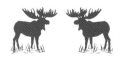

*The pride of the Rockies, the Indian Paintbrush (Castilleja maniata) is very flamboyant due to its vibrant red colour. Its stem varies from 20 to 30 cm and most bear only one flower. It can be found in all climatic zones, but prefers sunny, well drained slopes. Its colour can range from white and cream to yellow and pink as well as several shades of red. (above)*

*In the arctic, when the tundra turns red in autumn, one needs to wear dark sunglasses on a bright sunny day. In the Rocky Mountains, the situation is the same. As witness, this fiery red, red tundra by the Columbia Icefield. Jasper National Park. (left)*

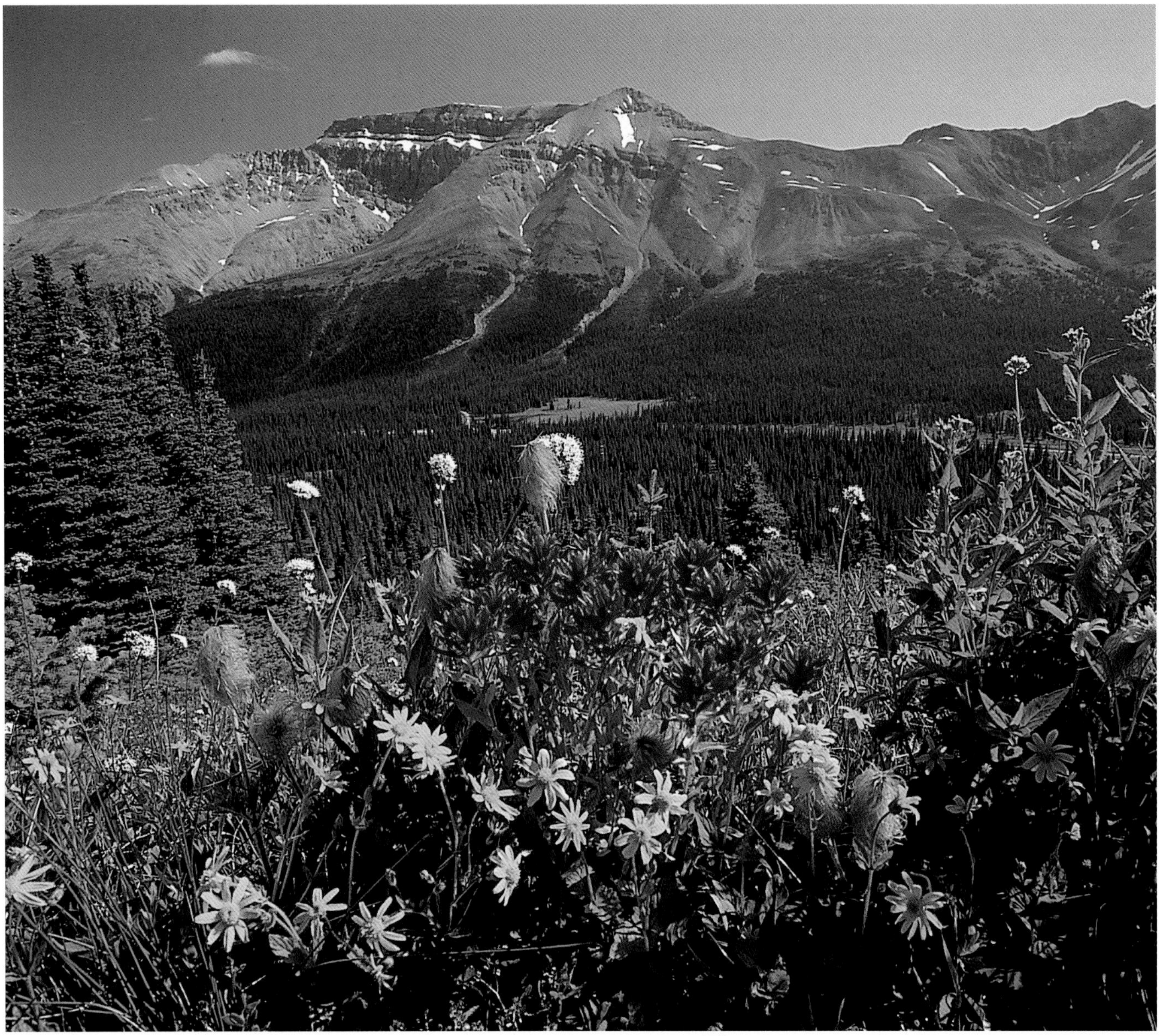

*The pristine and undisturbed ecosystem that still exists at the Bow Summit in Banff National Park. Sweet summer memories of long walks along nature trails through mountain meadows, can be yours for the asking. It is imperative that one stays on the trail, though, because the fragile alpine environment can be destroyed so very quickly.*

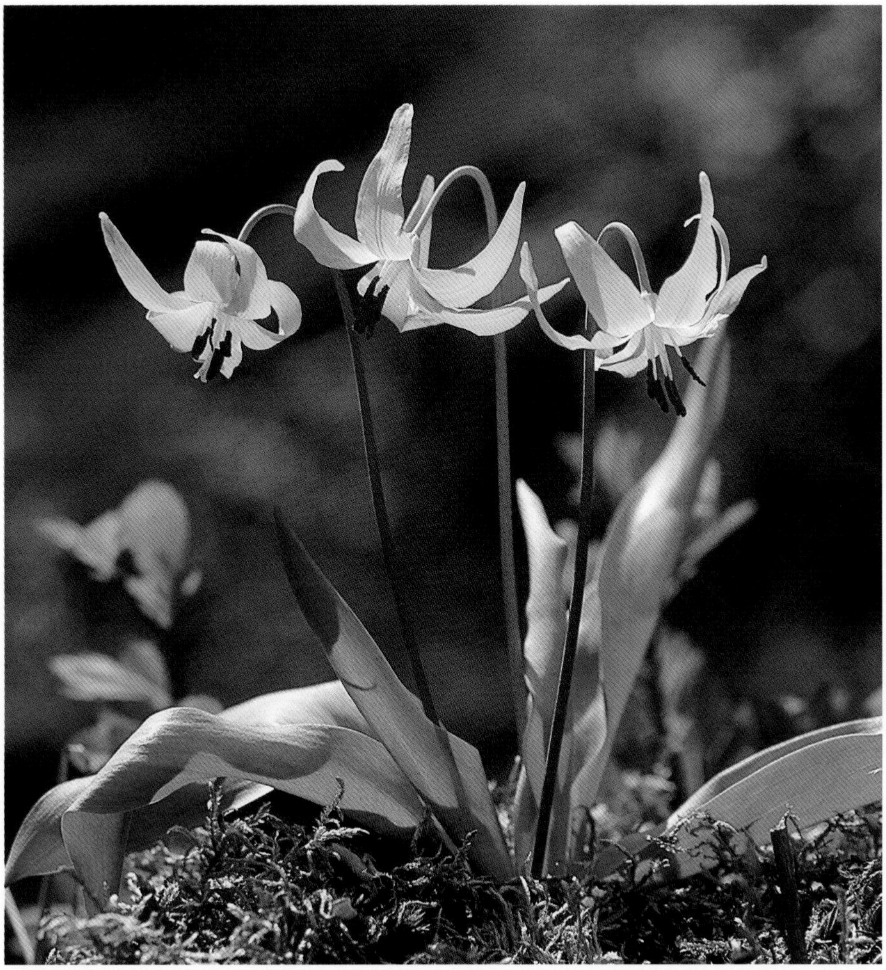

*A Liliaceae - the large Lily family represents nearly thirty species. One of the prettiest is-this harbinger of spring, the Glacier Lily (Erythronium grandiflorum). 25 cm in average height, it bears up to three bright flowers and can be found along moist alpine meadows, snowbeds and streams toward the end of May and into June. It is common throughout the western mountains.*

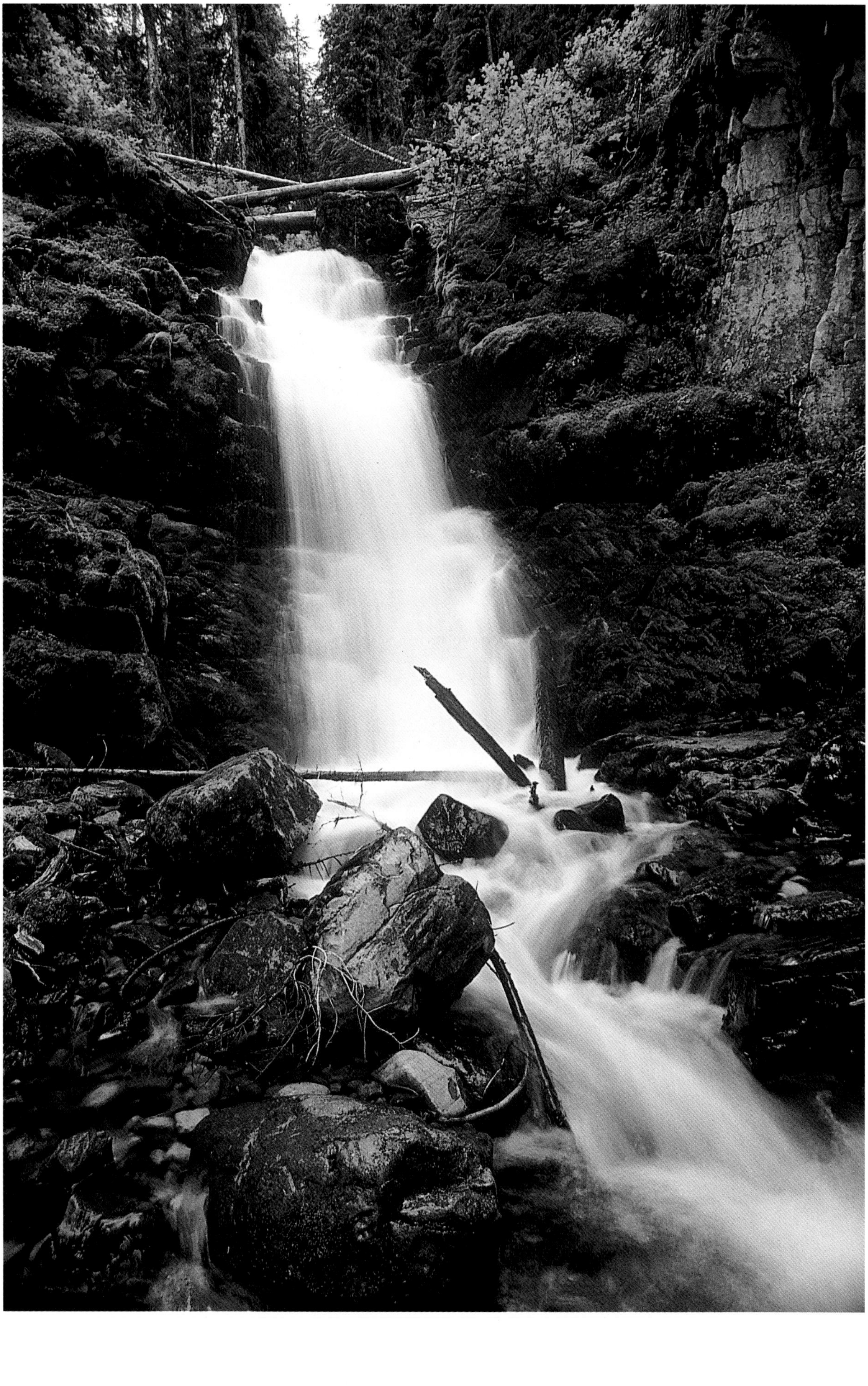

*A waterfall on Rawson Creek, originating at Rawson Lake, just south of Upper Kananaskis Lake. This is an ideal place to take a healthy, invigorating hike to recharge your spiritual batteries and keep you fit. (left)*

*The Hoary Marmot (Marmota ealigata) of North America is a member of the giant terrestrial squirrels group, along with the Woodchuck and Groundhog. The Marmot lives in an underground den and takes a prolonged nap from October to May. Here a Marmot family picnics in Yoho National Park. (below)*

*Lake O'Hara and Mary Lake (foreground) in Yoho National Park, are surrounded by spectacular, tall, glaciated mountains. With their easy access by road, large commercial lodge, large mountain hut and large campground, they attract many visitors. As a result, the area is abused and damaged, needing immediate care. (above)*

*Lower Waterfowl Lake is one of a few in the Mistaya River Valley. It is clean and pristine at the far end but littered and damaged along the highway. The mountain beneath these deep blue Alberta skies is Mt. Chephren (3266m). Banff National Park. (left)*

*A great variety of flowers and plants thrive on this sheltered slope at an elevation of 2600 m. "As we cleared another rocky ridge, suddenly a glorious alpine garden enveloped in front of our surprised eyes." - (author unknown). A hanging garden of Semiramis?(above)*

*On the way to Helen Lake and the Dolomite Pass in Banff National Park, a glorious alpine meadow sprawls across the valley. In August, the variety of flowers and colours astonishes visitors. Nature's performance fluctuates dramatically. One year it is first rate, but the next there may be few small flowers or even none at all. It is simply nature's cycle and the peculiarities of weather anomalies. Dolomite Peak (2782m) stands guard on the east side of the valley.(left)*

*High above the timberline, in a sheltered gully beside a small creek, a colourful little alpine garden basks in the sun.*

*Grass, flowers and other plantlife flourish in the rich, moist soil of this small well lit clearing in a dense Lodgepole Pine forest.*

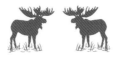

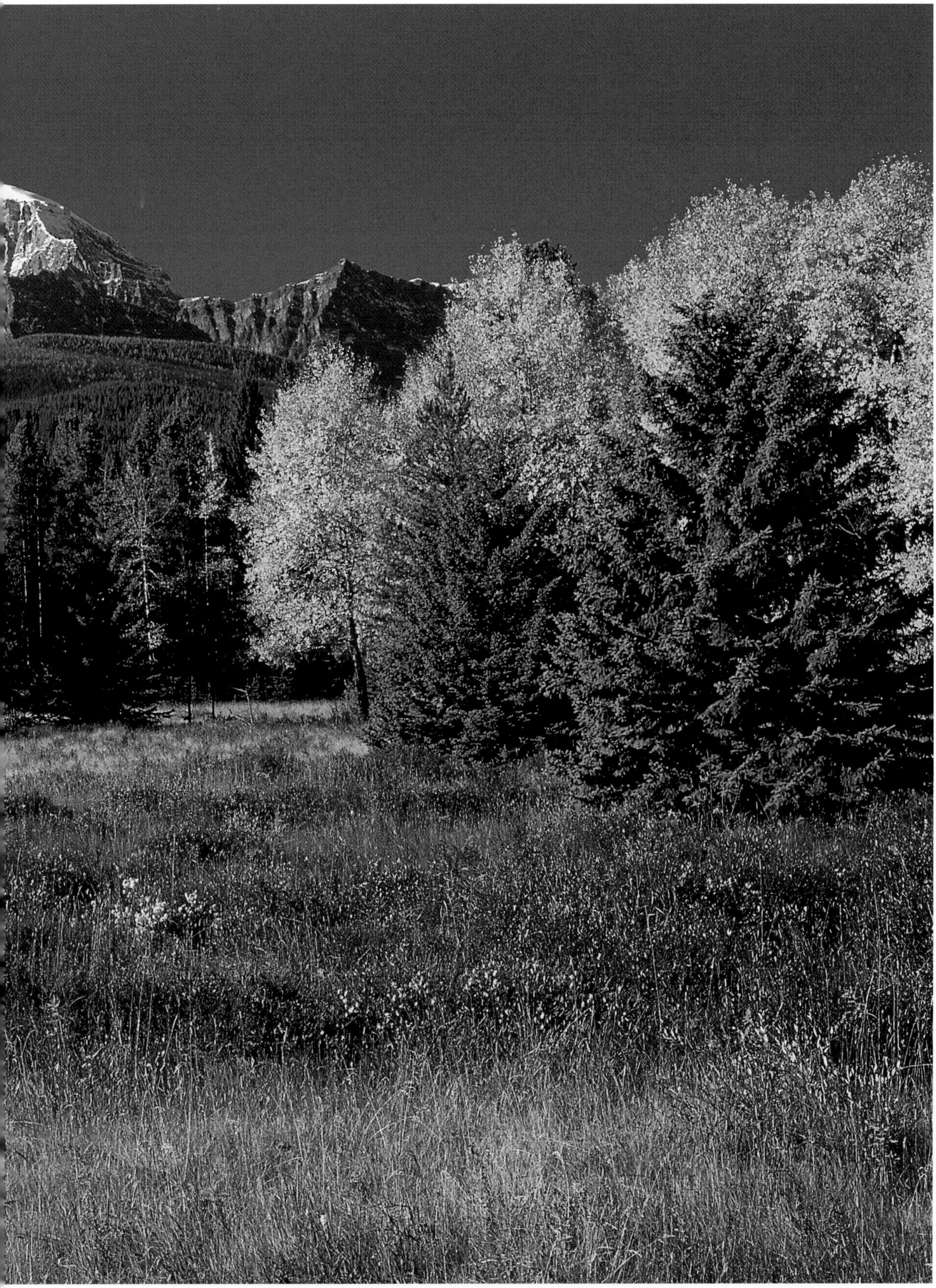

*A shrubby meadow in the Bow River Valley basks in the sun on a glorious autumn morning. Snow clad Storm Mountain (3161 m) guards the Alberta - British Columbia border. In Alberta the skies are always blue. Almost.*

*The Columbian Ground Squirrel (Spermophilus columbianus) guarding the entrance to his burrow. This fertile rodent is a food source for many predators and can be found throughout the region. (above)*

*Most likely, only a few hundred years ago, this place was sheathed in ice. Even now, Yoho Glacier is only three hundred meters away to the right. The rocky slope in the photo was carved and polished by the ice of the now declined glacier. Yoho National Park. (left)*

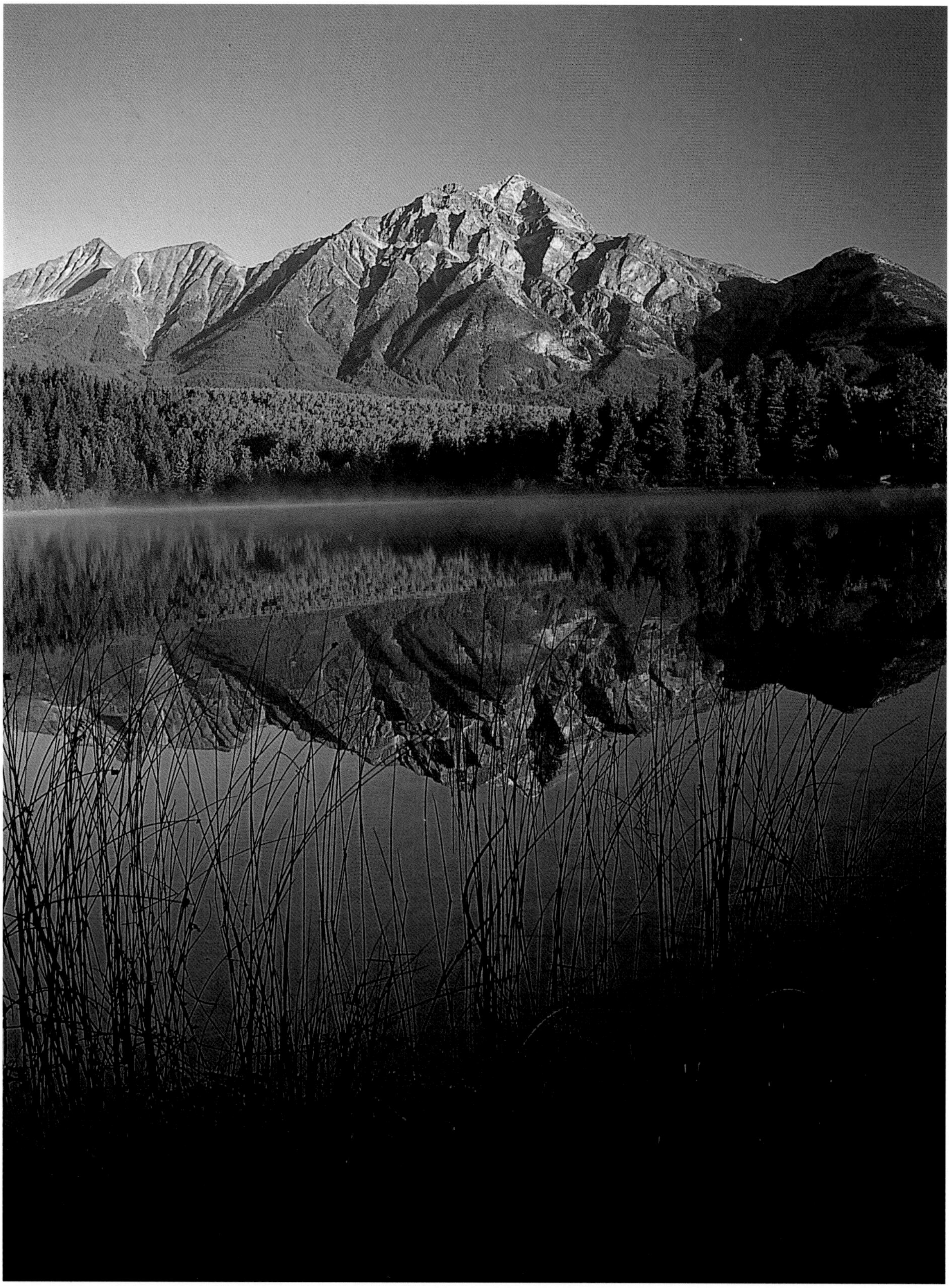

*The favourite scenic spot around Jasper, is Patricia Lake - shown here reflecting Pyramid Mountain (2766m). It is a stroke of good fortune to get the combination of blue skies, calm waters and the mountain's reflection at sunrise.*

## Wilderness and more ...

The moods of the mountains are expressed in many ways: mysterious hidden valleys; green, dark mountain forests; great swift rivers, torrents and streams; emerald green, and blue jewel-like lakes, tarns, and ponds; the majestic inhabitants of the mountain wilderness - from moose and wolves to chirping pika; all play an important part in maintaining the fragile web of continuing life.

Jagged, fearsome peaks, sheer walls and silvery ridges send shivers down our spines. Cascading glaciers and desolate icefields are ancient things that command respect and awe.

Amidst this mountain majesty, the most thrilling aspect of the Rockies is their lush, flowering meadows; the kaleidoscopic hues, the intricate shapes and the sheer delicacy of mountain flowers; the dazzling fragrances of herbs and flowers all combine to create a one-of-a-kind experience.

Mountain meadows are home to fauna seldom seen elsewhere. Heavenly mountain meadows are the heartbeat of the Rockies - masterpieces of nature's eternal creation. They are places to visit, respect, admire and leave undisturbed. The wild, green and pristine Rockies mean a healthy natural ecosystem - a green lungs for man and beast alike; a healthy environment for all to enjoy. The Rockies must remain green!

Now that you have looked through this book, you know what a special treasure the Canadian Rockies really are. Few places in the entire world can match it. These photographs present the totally wild and unspoiled mountains. Well, sort of. Sometimes, only a few feet from the "wild" in a photo, there is a power line, parking lot or large hotel. Sometimes it is difficult to take a "wild" photo without having some man-made object intrude: like a power line, highway or railway.

Regretfully, it must be said that the Rockies are quite devastated. Some areas in our National Parks can no longer be classified as wilderness. Continuing development and abuse by millions of visitors have taken their toll on this fragile ecosystem.

Today's fast-living society will tell you "it is not all that bad." "Let's build another hotel/road/golf course and bring in more tour buses. It won't make that much difference." Oh, really?

Look at what has happened at Bow Lake in Banff National Park. For five months each year, tour buses come to visit this beautiful lake. The toilets cannot accommodate the thousands of tourists, so expansion continues. Taking sewage away from holding tanks by truck is no longer possible because of the high volume. The solution: a huge underground sewage treatment system is built just by the shore of this spectacular lake .

The same dilemma faces most of the large developments in the Rockies. The Parks' rules and regulations are often ignored or misinterpreted. What is the government doing about this?

Maybe, when environmentalists and the public at large press hard and loudly enough, the government might wake up long enough to launch a multi-million dollar study into the situation. Maybe it will even consider the enquiry's recommendations. When the dust settles, very little will actually be done.

During the cold war communists were the enemy. With the cold war gone, the environmentally concerned seem to have taken their place. These "greens" are now the apparent targets of the system.

They are the only people who are trying to DO something to save what is left of this once beautiful, green planet.

The other side does just the opposite: destroying the environment just to make another dollar.

For them: pecunia non olet. Never!

If you feel that fighting the system is hopeless, a losing battle, there is another way to fight for a healthy environment.

Do the right thing yourself . Get your family, friends and neighbors to do so. Rules and laws are made to benefit some, not all . Read them intelligently and carefully and interpret them smartly.

For example: in some lakes within our National Parks, power boats are allowed. Ask yourself how the loon, duck or moose can make their homes there amidst all that human presence with its noise and pollution - in a National Park that was created to protect nature. The answer is that they don't live on that lake's area.

If the authorities are blind to these events, you don't have to be. Do not use your power boat in wilderness waters because it will destroy them.

We all know that some people use skidoos to chase and harass animals in the winter. Try to imagine what hardships an animal goes through in the wilderness during six months of winter. Only the basest of people would inflict even more hardship on such an animal.

Fewer and fewer wild flowers can be seen in areas populated by good old homo sapiens. In some areas, once plentiful flowers are now extinct due to illegal picking.

How can you save the mountain flowers? First, never pick any plant in a National Park or anywhere else. Second, report anyone you may see picking flowers. Flowers must complete their life cycle in order to reproduce.

It is very important not to litter in the wilderness. Throwing away a candy wrapper or pop can is not convenient - it is a wasteful and destructive mindset. When you go hiking, carry your garbage out of the park with you. It will only weigh a few ounces. Considerate and concerned people will pick up any litter they encounter and remove it from the wilderness. You can be one of them.

When you behave properly in the woods, you help the wilderness to survive. Be respectful and do not cause any damage. Remember, you are a guest there - a visitor. You are in the home of our wild friends and your behaviour should not disturb their lives.

People feed wild animals out of kindness, and with the best of intentions. It is a temptation that is hard to resist. However, feeding animals is against the law because it can make them dependent on human food and unable to forage for themselves. Some foods can make the animals sick. Most importantly, many animals are killed by cars as they hang around at roadside, looking for handouts. Please, never feed the wildlife.

We all know that many huge forest fires have been started by careless smokers. We also know that over 40,000 Canadians die each year because of smoking.

Our government could follow the lead of other civilized countries and pass laws prohibiting smoking by anyone under the age of twenty. Hiding behind the overinflated cliché of "freedom", the government would rather let 40,000 Canadians die than force them to save themselves. We are not allowed to drive a car before a certain age, where's the freedom in that?

This leads to a nagging question. When some product on the market is found to cause cancer, it is soon banned and vanishes from the shelves. Tobacco has been found to cause cancer and kills over a million people, worldwide, each year. Why is it still legal to buy tobacco at all? Perhaps this specific example tells us who really runs the world. (Hint: it's not the governments of the world.)

As you can see, nobody is going to help, advise or guide you. Killing for money is going on, on a global scale.

Only you can save yourself, if you are smart enough. Do not smoke. Make sure your children know what smoking does. You will save about $200,000 in your average non-smoking lifetime (can you imagine?)

And not only won't you be likely to die from cancer, or in a house fire, you won't be the cause of any devastating forest fires.

Are these not sufficient inducements to reject the irrational, ugly and dangerous habit of smoking?

There are many public and commercial facilities in our National Parks that should never have been built because they incite further development and commercialization while destroying the wilderness.

The best, possibly the only way to stop such things is to refuse to support them. If the money stops, the destruction stops.

The wilderness is supposed to be just that-wilderness! Wild. Natural. Pristine.

People used to think that Canada was so large that it would be impossible to destroy it. Today's reality is that the narrow strip of land along the U.S./Canada border is heavily populated and developed. In many areas, our environment is badly damaged.

We cut down trees faster than they can grow, because we waste paper products on a massive scale. A small group of visionaries are fighting a running battle with the not-so-noble people who would cut down every last tree to make a dollar. What can we do to help? A lot!

Many products are double, or even triple packed and many of those packages are half empty. To produce them, industry must use three times more cardboard (trees) than needed. To fight this mindless waste, simply do not buy overpackaged items and tell your store managers why you are boycotting these products. Write to the manufacturers and tell them, too.

If you live in the city where such wasteful companies operate, take them to small claims court and sue them for wasting natural resources and causing unnecessary pollution and garbage. You never know when you might run across a judge who is sympathetic to the green cause instead of big business.

Buy bulk food in one plastic bag which can be recycled. Buy only environmentally friendly products. Only then can you not blame yourself for the damage being caused to this planet.

Our health, our immune system, is only as good as the health of our planet. When nature is in ill health, damaged or destroyed, we will all follow the trend.

It is never too late to repair the wrongs of the past. This spring, plant the seeds of hope for our survival. Invest your heart and your savings into the promise of a better tomorrow. Plant 10 - 20 trees on your lot, or anywhere else you can. Plant the seeds of hope today for a healthy, happy and beautiful tomorrow.

# The Author

There are authors, artists, publishers, an entire industry, that will create any product that will sell and bring profit. Its message, its impact on society does not matter - money is all.

George Brybycin believes that a book, magazine or, indeed, any publication must have a positive, constructive influence on society. It must educate and inform as well as entertain and in that order. Otherwise, it is a waste of paper and a few hundred more dead trees.

Therefore, it is absolutely essential that Government subsidize all publications that are of value to society through substantial grants.

An ardent naturalist, George Brybycin tries to convey the message that "Nature is forever" is fast becoming "Nature is quickly vanishing."

Some misguided people call environmentalists alarmists - giving them a negative connotation. There is a clear, logical argument against that: every year, a few hundred species of flora and fauna vanish forever. The chain of nature, the interdependence of one species upon another, is broken. Ergo, more and faster damage will occur until...

How does one become an environmentalist?

From very early childhood, George's mother introduced him to the beautiful and gentle world of flowers, plants and trees - sparked in him interest and respect for these things.

As a small child, the author drew and painted nature. At the age of ten, he got into mountainscape photography while hiking as a Boy Scout.

And now after travelling the world, climbing hundreds of mountains and publishing twenty four books, George, still has not considered slowing down or changing subjects. Mountains, and photography are George's loves; his passions; his world.

Brybycin has always been a humble, frugal and non-materialistic man - happy with what he has. The only "greed" within him is the great desire for more knowledge, more wilderness and more good photographs to use in the publication of more books to share with those who have appreciated and supported his honest and enthusiastic creations.

"Nature lends herself to all men, but she gives herself only to a few" . (Francois Mauriac) George hopes that he is one of that lucky few.

To compensate for trees cut to produce paper for books, George Brybycin will continue to finance tree planting in Calgary.

A tree planted in Chicago, Frankfurt, Tokyo or Warsaw does the same thing - contribute to a global fresh air bank. Ergo, wherever you live, plant more trees on your property or donate money for tree planting.

Leave a noble green legacy for your children, friends and fellow man. Our badly damaged planet must became healthy and green once again.

Front cover: Bow Lake, Banff National Park.
Back cover: The Valley of the Ten Peaks, Banff National Park.
Page 1 Common Harebell (Campanula rotundifolia)
Page 2 By Bow Lake, Banff National Park.

This book was created in Alberta by Albertans.
Printed in Singapore by Khai-Wah-Ferco Pte. Ltd.
Text Editor: Sheldon Wiebe
Design: George Brybycin
Typesetting: K & H United Co.
First Edition 1997
ISBN 0-919029-25-6 Hardcover


For current list, please write to:
GB PUBLISHING, Box 6292, Station D,
Calgary, Alberta Canada T2P 2C9